Smile with Yoga

Fun, Mindful, and Engaging Yoga for Kids

I. Rekem

Illustrated by Alifstyle

Poetryoga

Printed in the United States of America

ISBN: 978-94-93054-00-4 eBook
ISBN: 978-94-93054-01-1 paperback

Published by Poetryoga® 2018

Website: www.smilewyoga.com
Email: contact@smilewyoga.com
Illustrated by Alifstyle
Stick figures by Hazuto Hima
Designed by Catherine Baduin

I. Rekem is the founder of Poetryoga, a specialized yoga brand for children. He is a
lifelong devotee of the ancient mind-body discipline as well as an entrepreneur,
a software engineer, a tutor, and a writer.

To my parents

Butterfly

Bottom on the floor, feet pressed together,
A butterfly is ready for any weather.
Starting as a caterpillar all squished and tight,
Now spreading its wings, what a beautiful sight.

Did you know?

A butterfly has four stages in its life cycle:
egg, caterpillar, pupa, and adult.

Cat

Eyes look down while back is arched,
Now you're a cat, ready to march.
To make this pose purrrrrfectly right,
Practice it consistently, day and night.

Did you know?

Cats are most active during the twilight hours: between sunset and full night and before sunrise. They have sharp night vision and need little light to find their way around.

Downward Dog

Head between your arms, hands to the ground,
Pull your feet up closely, but don't make a sound.
Dogs are faithful, loyal, and true,
Wagging their tails while jumping on you.

Did you know?

Dogs have a great sense of smell, up to 100,000 times better than a human's sense of smell. One of their favorite smells is of a familiar person.

Dolphin

With your arms shaped like a "V,"
Dive headfirst into the sea.
Dolphins speak with a special chatter,
Moving through the ocean like a hot knife through butter.

Did you know?

Dolphins give themselves names. They each have an individual whistle and recognize other dolphins' whistles, just like we recognize other people by their names. They take care of the sick and injured members of their pod and will not leave them behind. Aren't dolphins just adorable?!

Ragdoll

Legs closed as you bend down,
Arms limp to touch the ground.
Like a doll that bends this way,
You'll be much easier to put away.

Warrior II

Stretch your arms wide, bend the left knee,
Right leg back, straight as can be.
Balance is the key to doing it right,
Giving you perfect strength and might.

Flamingo

On one foot, standing tall,
Try not to wobble, try not to fall.
Flamingos are skinny in shades of pink,
Always near water, but not in your sink!

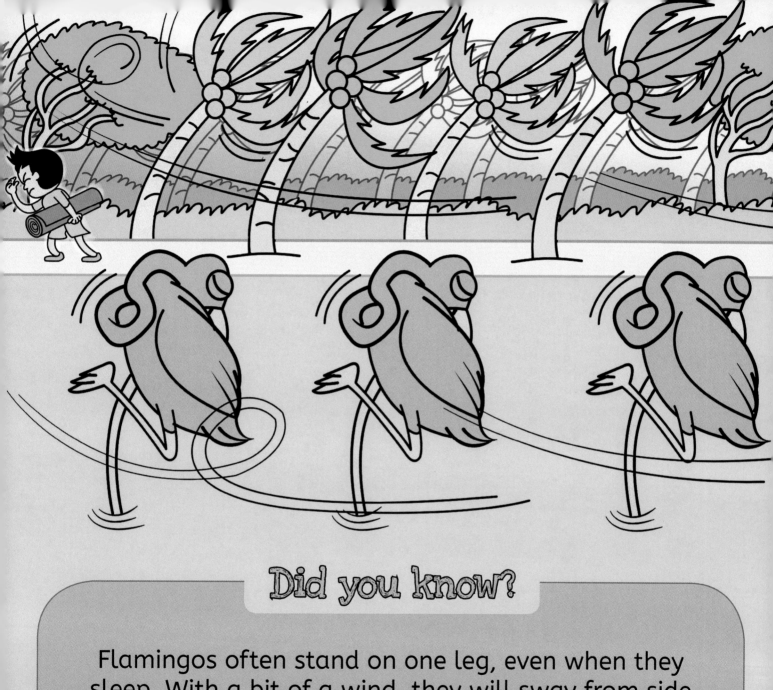

Did you know?

Flamingos often stand on one leg, even when they sleep. With a bit of a wind, they will sway from side to side but keep their balance.

Frog

Feet and hands on the ground,
Carefully looking all around.
If you were a frog you'd quickly spy
A juicy bug just flying by.

Did you know?

Frogs are amphibian: They live both on land and in water. Frogs start their lives as tadpoles in the water and come onto land as adults, although they will still visit the water occasionally.

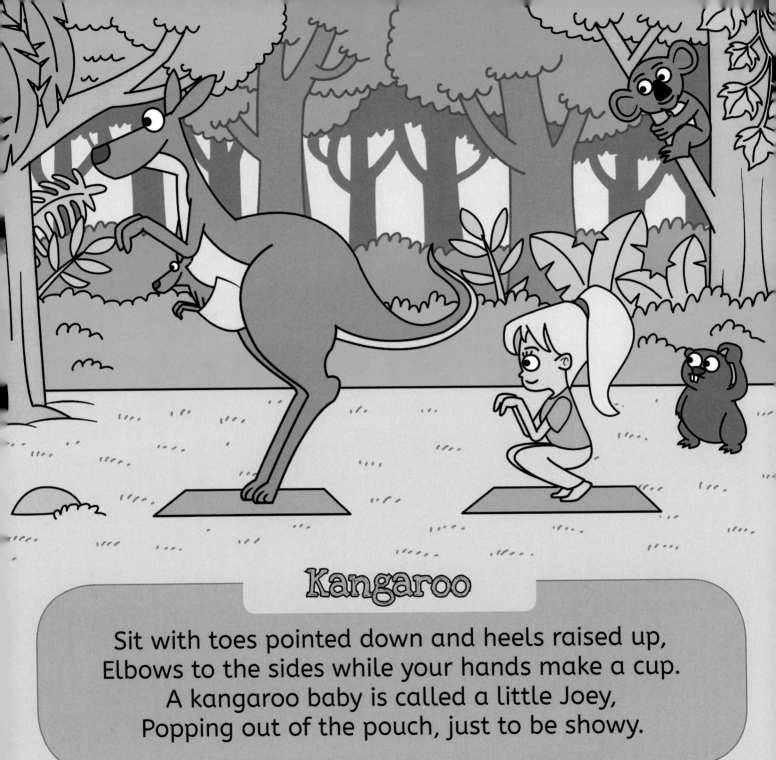

Kangaroo

Sit with toes pointed down and heels raised up,
Elbows to the sides while your hands make a cup.
A kangaroo baby is called a little Joey,
Popping out of the pouch, just to be showy.

Did you know?

Kangaroos can't walk or jump backward because of their muscular legs, big feet, and heavy tail.

Lion

Crouched like a lion in the tall grass,
Waiting for a zebra to finally pass.
You might get tired sitting in a bunch
If you had to wait so long for lunch.

Did you know?

Lions spend most of their time resting and sleeping, often as many as 20 hours a day.

Giraffe

On your knees with one hand low,
Stretch as high as you can go.
Have you ever heard a giraffe sing a song?
I'm sure it can with a neck so long!

Did you know?

Giraffes' spots are distinctive: Every giraffe has its own unique pattern. Just like giraffes, people are unique. Each one of us has a different pattern on our fingertips.
There is no one just like you!

Rainbow

Curved like a rainbow in the sky,
One leg bent and one arm high.
Red, orange, yellow, green, violet, indigo and blue...
This pose can be done even better by two.

Mermaid

One arm reaching above the sea,
As if to say, "Come look at me!"
Legs are not needed to make this motion,
Since mermaids swim deep in the ocean.

Pigeon

One leg behind, one tucked in front,
Arms on either side is the pose we want.
The pigeon always keeps moving ahead,
Just keep tossing him pieces of bread.

Did you know?

Pigeons have outstanding navigational abilities. They can find their way back home from a long distance or out of places they have never been before.

Flower

Sitting down, legs pulled to your tummy,
To a bumblebee, you look quite yummy.
Like a flower swinging in the breeze,
Sway from side to side, bending your knees.

Boat

With your bottom on the ground, pull your legs in close,
You're a boat sailing coast-to-coast.
Breathe in, breathe out, try not to think,
You do not want your boat to sink.

Snake

Lie on your tummy, your legs held flat,
Lift your head up so you can see where you're at.
Raising up their heads and listening to the flute,
Snakes are charmed by the gentle "toot, toot, toot."

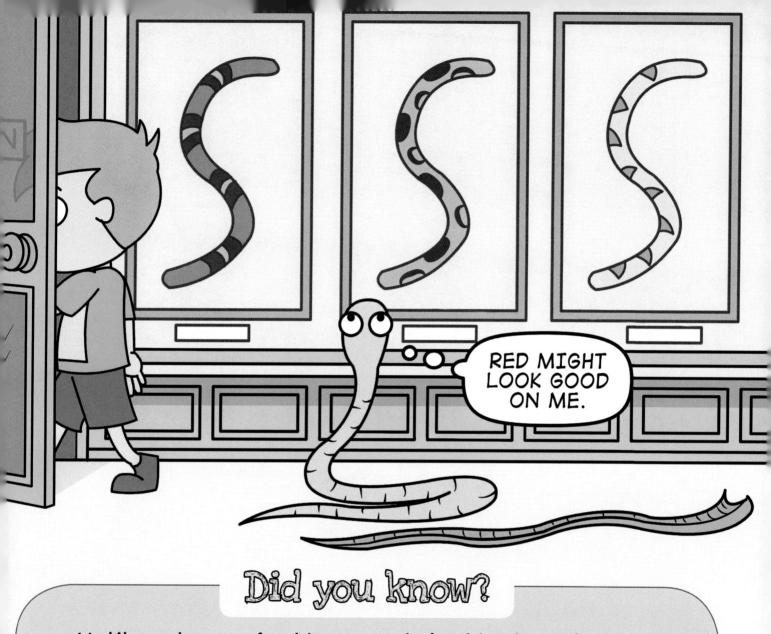

Did you know?

Unlike a human's skin, a snake's skin doesn't grow with its body. Snakes shed their skin periodically, when it has become too small and a new layer has grown underneath.

Camel

Like a camel on its knees,
Arching backward with ankles squeezed.
If a camel could really stretch this way,
His hump might finally go away.

Did you know?

Camels' humps store fat, not water! The fat can be broken down and used for nutrition. This allows camels to go without water for days and without food for months.

Bridge

Head, arms, and feet on the floor,
Raise your back. Is it sore?
Here is a bridge, long and straight,
On top it carries some extra weight!

Relaxation

Here we are at the last pose,
Lying down with eyes closed.
Don't move, speak, hiccup, or jiggle,
Don't sneeze, yawn, burp, or giggle!

The Poses - Step-by-Step

Butterfly

1. Begin seated on the ground with your knees bent to the sides and bring the bottoms of your feet together.
2. Slide your feet in close to your body. Hold on to your feet and sit up nice and tall. Take a deep breath in and out. You can move your knees up and down like a butterfly's wings.

Cat

1. Start on your hands and knees, like a table. Take a big breath in.
2. As you breathe out, round your back, reaching it to the sky, and tuck your chin toward your chest. On your next breath in, come back to where you started, with a flat back.

Downward Dog

1. Start on your hands and knees, like a table.
2. Tuck your toes, spread your fingers wide, and press down into the ground with strong arms as you lift your hips to the sky. Keep your arms and legs straight, so your body makes a triangle shape. You can bend your knees a bit to keep the back flat.
3. Your heels may or may not touch the ground, but with practice, reaching the ground will get easier. Breathe in and out a few times before lowering your knees back down to the ground.

Dolphin

1. Begin on your hands and knees, like a table.
2. Lower your elbows to the ground and interlace your fingers.
3. Tuck your toes and lift your hips to the sky. Straighten your legs; you can bend your knees a bit to keep the back flat. Let your head relax down toward the ground, hanging between your arms, as you look between your feet. When you are ready to come out of the pose, gently lower your knees back to the ground.

RagDoll

1. Start standing up straight.
2. Bend over at your waist to let your head and arms hang toward the ground.
3. You can stay still, or you can gently sway from side to side as you breathe deeply in and out. To finish, come slowly back up to standing.

Warrior II

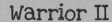

1. Begin standing with your feet wide apart. Turn your right foot to point out to your right side, and bend your right knee so it lines up over your right ankle.
2. Keep your left leg straight and stretch your arms out to your sides at shoulder height, like you're making a "T" with your upper body. Turn your head to look out over your right hand, and take steady breaths. Switch and do the pose on the other side.

Flamingo

1. Start standing up tall.
2. To help with this balance pose, look straight ahead and pick an unmoving spot to stare at. Now lift your right foot behind you, keeping your knees close together.
3. Reach behind you with your right hand to catch your lifted right foot, and stretch your left arm straight up over your head. Breathe in and out as you keep your gaze fixed on the spot ahead. Then slowly lower your left arm and right leg back down. Repeat the pose on the other side.

Frog

1. Begin standing up straight and tall with your feet slightly turned out.
2. Sink down into a squat with your knees wide apart and your hands on the ground in front of you.
3. Sit up nice and tall, looking straight ahead as you breathe slowly in and out.

Kangaroo

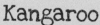

1. Crouch all the way down so your bottom is close to the ground. Lift your heels off the ground so you are balancing on your tiptoes.
2. Bring your arms in by your sides and your hands up in front of you, palms facing out. Curve your hands into little paws.
3. Look straight ahead and take five little hops on your toes.

Lion

1. From a kneeling position, sit back so your bottom is on your feet and your hands are on the ground in front of you. Keep your arms straight.
2. Take a big breath in. Open your eyes wide and look up. Open your mouth wide and stick your tongue out. As hard as you can, push all the air back out through your wide-open mouth.

Bridge

1. Begin lying on your back with your arms by your sides and your palms facing down.
2. Bend your knees so they point up to the ceiling and slide your feet in close to your bottom. Take a deep breath in.
3. As you breathe out, press down with your feet and your hands, lifting your hips and back off the ground. Stay here for a few in-and-out breaths before gently lowering back down to the ground.

Rainbow

1. Begin kneeling on the ground with your hips lined up over your knees and your arms reaching straight out to your sides like a "T."
2. Reach your left hand down to the ground on your left side and stretch your right arm up toward the sky.
3. Straighten out your right leg, keeping your right foot on the ground. Reach your right arm over your head so it touches your ear. Breathe in and out a few times before repeating on the other side.

Mermaid

1. Begin sitting down with your knees bent and your feet flat on the ground in front of you. Support yourself with your hands on the ground behind you.
2. Slide both feet over to the right side of your body, letting your knees rest on the ground, pointing to the left side.
3. Stretch your left arm up to the sky and rest your right hand on your right foot. Take a few deep in-and-out breaths before switching to the other side.

Pigeon

1. Start on your hands and knees.
2. Bring your left foot forward with your knee bent. Wiggle that foot across the front of your body until your left lower leg rests on the ground.
3. Stretch your right leg straight out behind you and sit up nice and tall. Breathe slowly in and out a few times before coming back up to your hands and knees. Repeat the pose with your right leg forward and your left leg behind you.

Giraffe

1. Start on your hands and knees.
2. Keep your right hand on the ground and reach your left arm toward the sky. Look toward the sky and breathe deeply a few times before lowering your hand back to the ground. Repeat the pose on the other side.

Boat

1. Begin sitting on the ground with your knees bent and your feet on the ground in front of you. Put your hands on the ground behind you.
2. Keeping your back nice and straight, lean back a little, bending your elbows until you can balance on your bottom. Lift your feet one at a time until both are off the ground.
3. Stretch both of your arms out in front of you so you are balancing only on your bottom, feet raised. Stay here for a few slow breaths before bringing your feet and arms back down.

Snake

1. Start lying down on your belly with your legs stretched out straight behind you. Reach your arms behind you over your bottom.
2. Breathe in and lift your head and chest up, rolling your shoulders back. Stay here for a few slow in-and-out breaths before lowering back down.

Flower

1. Begin sitting on the ground with your knees bent out to the sides and the bottoms of your feet touching together in front of you.
2. Reach your hands under your knees and pull them through so your knees are resting on your arms. Open your hands and point your palms toward the sky.
3. Gently lean back and lift your feet off the ground until you are balancing on your bottom. If you pick a spot in front of you to look at, it will help you stay balanced. Take a few slow in-and-out breaths before gently bringing your feet back down to the ground and unwinding your arms.

Camel

OR

1. Begin kneeling with your shins on the ground and your hips lined up over your knees.
2. Put your hands on your hips to support your back. Press your pelvis forward and look up to the sky. Breathe deeply in and out a few times before straightening back up.
3. For the harder version, reach your arms behind you until your hands rest on your heels. Look up to the sky and lift your chest, pushing your hips forward to keep them lined up over your knees. Breathe deeply in and out a few times before releasing your hands and sitting your bottom down on your feet. Straighten up.

Relaxation

1. Lie down on your back, feet stretched out in front of you. Straighten out your arms, reaching toward your feet, and turn your palms up to face the sky. Let your feet fall open away from each other. Close your eyes and let your body relax completely.

Games and Activities

1. **Downward Dog Tunnel**: Line up shoulder to shoulder with all your fellow yogis except one, and get into downward-dog pose, forming a tunnel. The one remaining yogi crawls through the tunnel like a puppy, emerges on the other side, and hops into downward dog pose at the end of the line, calling out *"next playful puppy on the way!"* At that signal, the yogi at the front of the tunnel breaks off and crawls through, joins the line, and gives the signal for the yogi in front to break off, continuing the game until everyone has played the puppy.

2. **Wacky Kangaroo**: Kangaroos can't walk or jump backward. Can you walk backward? Choose a partner, find a clear path without obstacles, and walk backward as your partner navigates. Then change places. If you find it too easy, you can try hopping backward.

3. **Create Your Own**: If there were an "eggplant pose," what would it look like? Demonstrate your version of the pose. How about the "noodle pose"?

4. **Pigeon's-Eye View**: Pigeons are great navigators. Can you navigate like a pigeon?

   - Which landmarks do you use to find your way when you go outside?

   - On your next trip outside, look for new landmarks: a tall building, a bench in the park, or a tree on the street corner.

   If you add new places to your mental list every time you go outside, you can navigate like a pigeon!

5. **Jungle Concert**: Choose a yoga pose and perform it while making a sound related to the name of that pose.

6. **Flower Garden**: Sit in a circle and do the flower pose while holding hands with your neighbors. You can sway from side to side, or sing cheerfully -- just be a happy, colorful flower!

7. **Yogi Says**: The leader gets into a yoga pose, and you copy it – but only if the leader says "*Yogi says*"! If you get into the pose without the "yogi says," you have to demonstrate whatever funny pose the leader calls out. If you don't know it, make it up!

8. **Resting Lion**: Lions are aware of their surroundings even when resting. Can you be a resting lion? Sit outside or close to a window, without any distractions, and listen to the sounds. What voices and noises do you hear? Can you name them?

9. **Yoga Freeze Dance**: While the leader plays music, dance around the room. When the leader stops the music and calls out a yoga pose, stop dancing and get into that pose as fast as you can!

10. **Yoga Challenge**: When the leader calls out a body part, get into a yoga pose in which that body part touches the ground. For example, if the leader calls out "two hands," you could do a pose like frog, lion, or bridge. If you can't think of any yoga pose, you can invent one that fits the criteria – but you have to invent a name for it, too!